USING REWARDS WISELY

Jenny Mosley & Helen Sonnet

Permission to photocopy

This book contains materials which may be reproduced by photocopier or other means for use by the purchaser. The permission is granted on the understanding that these copies will be used within the educational establishment of the purchaser. The book and all its contents remain copyright. Copies may be made without reference to the publisher or the licensing scheme for the making of photocopies operated by the Publishers' Licensing Agency.

Using Rewards Wisely
MT10017
ISBN-13: 978 1 85503 408 2
ISBN-10: 1 85503 408 5
© Jenny Mosley and Helen Sonnet
All rights reserved
First published 2006

Printed in the UK for LDA
Abbeygate House, East Road, Cambridge, CB1 1DB, UK

Contents

Introduction

Why do we use rewards with children? Some people get very indignant just at the thought of them. Arguments against rewards include these:

☆ Children should behave anyway and shouldn't be rewarded for doing so.

☆ Rewards only teach children to please others.

These are counter to what we know about healthy psychological and moral growth, and are contrary to what we know about how children learn and how self-image is constructed. Thinking about what giving rewards wisely may do for individuals and the school community raises the following points:

☆ Children know that the school is a social culture that values and encourages particular behaviours and actions and discourages others.

☆ Children's attention is focused on the positive aspects of a school's ethos and they learn that effort and pro-social behaviour receive positive attention.

☆ Children know what is expected of them and how to interact peacefully in a school community.

☆ Children learn that all actions have consequences, some of which are enjoyable and positive.

☆ Children understand that life is about making choices and learn ways to evaluate their own behaviour.

☆ Rewards provide crucial feedback needed to build healthy self-esteem and self-efficacy.

☆ Rewards are a natural way of celebrating personal, social and academic efforts.

All successful child-rearing practices lead children towards independence, and the best models of reward giving are no different. In this book, we shall introduce a rewards system that begins with the adult community of a school clarifying what is praiseworthy, by reinforcing the positive efforts of children through a system of sanctions and rewards. The aim is for rewards to move from being extrinsic to intrinsic and internalised. This is achieved by enabling them to reward each other, and then to self-evaluate and reward themselves. Through this process, school values become owned by the children as individuals and as a group.

The thinking behind using rewards

This book will help you explore the rewards available and show you how to use them effectively. It will help you to think ahead and be proactive, not reactive. Your skill in administering rewards is crucial, which is why a wide range is described, such as:

☆ celebrating the attainment of Tiny, Achievable, Tickable Targets by individual children;

☆ focusing on one school Golden Rule by a class for a given time;

⭐ responding to a clear whole-school focus on creating positive lunchtimes.

Any occasion that is recognised with a reward indicates to the children what the wider school community cares deeply about. In a study by Jeremy Swinson and Alex Harrop of Liverpool John Moores University, the following positive effects of rewarding good behaviour were found:

⭐ an improvement in on-task activity in lessons;

⭐ a decrease in the level of teacher interventions for poor behaviour in lessons.

For rewards to be truly effective, they need to be consistent. You will usually start the term with enthusiasm and good intentions, armed with loads of rewards, but teaching is a demanding and busy profession and it is easy to run out of energy, enthusiasm, and even stickers. Your children may not comment to you on this drop-off, but don't delude yourself. They will have noticed that the rewards have stopped, and they are likely to draw the conclusion that you have run out of good will and passion for the school values or Golden Rules, and have lost interest in rewarding their efforts.

Developing a school rewards and sanctions policy will help you to be consistent in your use of rewards. This policy should include details of what sorts of rewards are to be used, what things will be rewarded, how successes are to be shared with the school community, and who will monitor the system. The policy should be reviewed regularly by a designated staff member to keep it fresh, vibrant and at the front of the minds of staff.

If children have their efforts recognised by frequent and regular praise, they build a healthy and positive self-image and are more likely to mature into optimistic adults – who don't crave praise and encouragement and are able to bounce back from disappointments and to learn from mistakes, rather than being crushed by them.

Rewards from adults let children know that they are succeeding at something they are doing, whether this is work, behaviour or relationships.

Rewards to individuals fall into two main groups:

☆ 'encouragers' aimed at telling children they are on the right track and help them to keep up the good effort;

☆ 'specials' that signify a child has done something particularly outstanding.

Encouragers are frequent, small rewards, such as stickers, ink stamps and verbal praise; specials are tangible and public, such as certificates, head teacher's tea parties and letters home.

Rewards given to a class or group tend to be cumulative and to reward the children for communal progress in working together to achieve a specific class target or targets.

Ensure that all children in your class receive a baseline level of encouragers and specials. Pay particular attention to the quiet majority of children whom we often describe as the 'well-behaved middle plodders'. The brightest children are aware that they stand out because of their academic success, and challenging children and those with specific difficulties usually receive praise as part of their special provision. The calm, quiet children who keep the rules and work conscientiously are often overlooked. They create the atmosphere in which everyone else can flourish, and rewarding their consistent efforts will strengthen the ethos that is such a crucial indicator of your success as a community.

Rewards are the building blocks on which to found systems that enable children to praise and reward each other. Peer praise is particularly effective and positive when directed at children who do not normally receive much attention from classmates. It enables them to experience the admiration of the children around them, which can be truly uplifting and motivating. In addition, it is important to ensure that children learn the art of self-praise by giving them opportunities to reflect on their own progress and to reward themselves in ways that are personally satisfying.

Types of reward

Verbal praise

The words you use can be a powerful ally in the classroom, or leave a trail of hurt and destruction. Choose them carefully. Making good news public by using verbal praise shows a child that you have noticed and appreciated their efforts, and allows everyone around them to find out that they have done well, reinforcing the act that receives positive regard.

Keep your praise specific so the child, and the wider community, are made aware of what is praiseworthy and can choose to repeat it in the future. Be alert, and focus on the acts that you appreciate and that support the school ethos. For example:

☆ 'That is very neat writing, Ashanti. Every word is on the line. Well done.'

☆ 'You stood calmly when you were lining up.'

☆ 'Well done for walking away when Jasmine called you an unkind name.'

A school is a social community. Use this when it comes to verbal praise. You can utilise the presence of other adults and ensure that news of a child's success reaches a wider audience. You could send a child into a colleague's classroom to show them good work or to tell them good news about their behaviour. If another adult is present in your classroom or another part of the school when you are praising a child, tell them about what you are praising the child for. Such small actions can have long-lasting effects.

Make the most of a moment of success by praising it loudly.

This method works when praising the whole class too, helping to build them up when they do something well and generating a positive group dynamic. Once again, use specific terms to address the children, such as these:

☆ 'A huge thank you to all of you for sitting quietly in assembly.'

☆ 'Well done. You are working together and sharing equipment very thoughtfully.'

Beware of non-specific praise that is based on personal traits. Such comments can lead other children to avoid difficult tasks and to fear failure. For example:

☆ 'You're good at this.'

☆ 'I'm proud of you.'

Accompanying your verbal praise with positive physical gestures can be very encouraging. A smile, a confirming nod, a pat on the shoulder or a thumbs-up will let children know that you are appreciative of their efforts. You know yourself that a big smile has the capacity to brighten your day and create a feeling of good will in you. Try to use it more frequently, and you will be amazed at the positive effect it has. Such physical gestures can be used on their own effectively.

Most children love to be praised, especially in front of others. However, for some children with low self-esteem, verbal praise in front of others can be terrifying and failure is a much more comfortable option. It is better to find a time to praise these children quietly when others are busy. Alternatively, you could praise such a child to another adult when the child is close enough to overhear your commendation and does not need to react to it publicly. If it is difficult to find such opportunities, stick a sticker into a child's book to reward good work, or put it in their drawer – with a note explaining what it is for if it is not for good work. Remember to persevere, even if the child does not appear to respond.

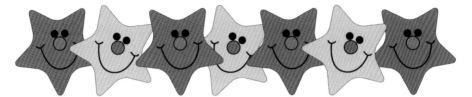

Stickers

Most children love to be given a sticker. When a child has a sticker on their top, they are showing everyone that they have done something praiseworthy. Stickers are a valuable talking point, enabling other members of the school community to engage in conversation about what the sticker signifies. They also give opportunities for more verbal praise, if appropriate.

Stickers, however, must be used with care. They should not be given out indiscriminately or overused, particularly those that have generic, rather than specific, wording.

As with verbal praise, it is best to award stickers that have specific commendations, such as these:

☆ 'I did brilliantly in the spelling test.'

☆ 'I read well today.'

☆ 'I got my numbers right.'

☆ 'Lovely handwriting.'

☆ 'Fantastic listening today.'

☆ 'I was polite today.'

Many stickers available from educational suppliers are suitable for use in schools. Some are of a general graphical nature. Some suppliers offer stickers with specific comments on relating to achievements and targets. LDA publish a range with comments such as these:

☆ 'Well done for staying calm.'

☆ 'We like your table manners.'

☆ 'I have been honest.'

☆ 'Well done for tidying up.'

See the Resources section on page 32.

Suppliers such as SuperStickers offer you customised stickers to meet your own needs. These may be ordered from www.superstickers.com; following the online instructions to create reward stickers with images and text of your choice. This helps you to promote a particular skill or behaviour. If you conduct Circle Times, you could have a session involving the children in choosing the text for the customised stickers.

Give each child a chart, bookmark or booklet to stick their stickers in and record achievements. Once a child has filled all the spaces, they could receive a particularly eye-catching certificate (see page 32).

Stampers

Pre-inked stampers are a quick and easy way to commend work. There are many to choose from. A number of companies offer a similar service for customised stampers as for stickers. There are ready-made stampers to commend good work, positive behaviour, improvement in specific areas, lunchtime successes and good homework. You can buy stamp stacks of three to five different stampers that offer a range of messages.

Stampers are a useful means of praise because they please children and convey quick, eye-catching messages to parents or carers. For example, a stamper that says 'I achieved the learning objective' shows the progress a child has made, whilst the message 'My teacher helped me today' indicates to a parent areas where a child may need further support.

To help children develop self-motivation, you can let them choose the stamp for a particular achievement and allow them the empowering task of stamping their own work. If you intend to do the stamping yourself, tell the children before they begin their work that you will be looking to see who has tried really hard as they will be getting one of your special stamps in their books.

Certificates

The great appeal of certificates is that the best ones have attention-grabbing graphics and look official. This gives them value for children. LDA produce a range that cover specific aspects of school life (see Resources section on page 32).

Certificates can be given out in a special ceremony which provides a whole-school audience for recipients.

There are certificates to celebrate such things as good work, achieving a target and regular attendance. There are also certificates for specific awards such as Pupil of the Week and Head Teacher's Award. Some can be used to recognise progress in particular subjects; whilst others are graded for levels of success, such as gold, silver and bronze.

Certificates can be sent home with the child or in the post. This provides the opportunity for them to be displayed so that visitors can see and comment on them. You could laminate certificates to enhance their display potential and longevity.

Keep a checklist to make sure that every child in your class receives a certificate during the school year.

Create your own rewards

Some schools hold a head teacher's tea party to which selected children are invited each week for a drink and a biscuit. This is a chance for the head teacher to chat with children about their work and school life. This can seem a huge privilege as the head teacher's room may be regarded as a special place to visit. You can increase the sense of occasion by making special invitations and allowing them to wear special clothes for the day rather than school uniform.

A special reward that also gives children responsibility is allowing them to visit a class of younger children, either to play a game with someone or to help. Such rewards need not take up much time and the time taken is more than saved by reduced time needed to tackle issues of disruption and challenging behaviour.

Special rewards can be particularly useful when they are part of a behaviour-management programme. Changing behaviour is very difficult and children who are really trying to achieve this deserve recognition. Helping the caretaker is popular as it gives the child a sense of accomplishment in serving the school, as do photocopying, tidying or sorting equipment.

On rare occasions you can offer a very desirable personal reward, such as a visit to a local café to have an ice cream with a member of staff significant for that child. This could be the incentive for a child to try hard for an agreed period, such as half a term. The child could ask a friend to accompany them. In choosing special rewards, canvass the children for ideas. You may be surprised at their suggestions; things you would consider mundane or ordinary can, unexpectedly, prove to be real winners with them.

Special child of the week award

There are many variations on the award in which one child is mentioned for commendation and recognition. Such an award is a valuable means of providing a positive focus for each child, and is crucial for those who may be in danger of being overlooked. A special-child award can boost the self-esteem of children who do not see themselves as successful or popular. Make sure *every* child experiences such an award during the school year.

One version of this is to have a Child of the Week display in your classroom. Each week a different child is chosen. Their picture is displayed on the board. Other children are invited to write a positive sentence about them on a slip of paper, and these are displayed around the photograph. Throughout the week, the chosen child has

certain privileges. For example, they are allowed to be first in line when queuing, granted special responsibilities in the form of jobs (such as taking the register to the office), and given the choice of a circle game. At the end of the week, you can select a few other children to read out the positive statements from the display and then the whole class gives the child a round of applause. This is a useful way of encouraging peer feedback and giving the other children the means to reward class members. It encourages empathy and builds a sense of the class as a caring community where children learn to take turns at being in the limelight.

Self-praise

Current thinking recognises that self-praise is a fundamental aspect of healthy self-esteem. Children should be encouraged to recognise, appreciate and applaud themselves when they have done something well. This is not immodesty but valuable self-assessment. We all have the right to be pleased with a job well done.

One way to develop this awareness is to give each child one sticker or star a week. They choose one thing that they consider to be their best effort to award themselves the star for. Some write an explanation beside the sticker, such as 'I awarded myself this star because I sat quietly and got on with this work while other people were talking around me.' If they are proud of an instance of behaviour in the week, they can draw a picture of their behaviour, add the sticker, and present the picture during a Circle Time. This can help them work to improve in areas where they can see they are not reaching the desired standard. This helps them to develop self-motivation, and ensures that the will to succeed matures and is prompted less by the need to receive praise and more by the need to strive and excel because of the satisfaction of achievement.

Each child can be given a scrapbook in which to stick their best items of work during the year. You can use this to discuss whether a piece of work has reached the desired standard, encouraging them to be honest and discriminatory. Some children may want to include every piece of work in their scrapbook in order to fill it up quickly, while others may never deem anything they do good enough. Helping children to develop a balanced judgement of their work is a valuable way of making them realistic in their expectations of themselves.

Self-assessment is an important part of children's development and of the life of successful schools. Children should be asked to evaluate a piece of work honestly and decide on its standard or how hard they tried when they produced it. Some schools use charts or forms for children to provide this feedback. This method can be simplified if a child is able to award themselves a star, sticker or grade as appropriate. The strategy helps those who find it easier to record something than to tell others about their accomplishments. Using a chart to assess progress also provides a visual record so the child can see how well they have done over a period of time.

Name   **Carlton**

For   **careful presentation**

You could utilise your Circle Times by including a round with the following sentence stem:

'One thing I did well this week was . . .'

Discuss with the children before you begin what they might choose to say. They could refer to work they have produced, behaviour they were proud of or a helpful act. Give the children a minute to think about what they will say before you begin the round. When all have spoken, tell them that they all deserve a clap and invite the whole class to applaud themselves.

If you have a child or children in your class who you think may have difficulty in deciding on something to complete their sentence with, you could remind them of something before the Circle Time begins.

A good-work board also allows children to develop self-evaluation skills. Each child is allowed to select a piece of work during each term to display on the board for one day. The child explains to the class why they have made this particular choice and then other children are invited to make positive comments about it.

Peer praise

If you have a strong commitment to creating a caring community in your classroom, building a culture of peer praise is essential. It helps children to learn that they do not need to look exclusively to adults for positive feedback. There are many strategies to use. Children can take turns to lead awards ceremonies which can be included in a weekly Circle Time. Another Circle Time strategy is to give one child three stickers. They award three classmates a sticker each, stating the reason why. The children should be encouraged to be discriminatory and not to opt for close friends.

Children could also nominate candidates for the head teacher's award, explaining the reason why in an assembly and placing the sticker on the child's sweatshirt, if appropriate.

Using a Golden Book and a Golden Chair encourages peer praise. For the former, a large scrapbook is covered in gold paper. Each week a different child's name is written on a page – along with a photograph, if available. The teacher starts by writing a positive comment about the child and then invites their classmates to write further comments on slips of paper to be glued in. When these have all been assembled, the child reads through the page of positive statements. This also serves as a record to refer to when times are harder for a child.

The child whose turn it is to be recorded in the Golden Book is also invited to sit on the Golden Chair. Other children ask them questions about their hobbies, interests and memorable occasions in their life as a way of getting to know them better. The session can end with applause.

Another strategy is to use a Golden Nominations Board. At the start of a week, choose a criterion for that week's nominations. Children are then asked to nominate a classmate who they think exhibit this quality. If you have several nominations, you can discuss who from the list deserves special recognition. If necessary, you can vote on the matter. Criteria could include:

✰ good behaviour;

✰ helpfulness;

✰ hard work;

✰ cheerfulness.

Make sure that each child appears on the board over the course of the year. Select categories carefully and drop subtle hints before you ask for nominations. For example, in the week prior to asking for nominations for cheerfulness, you might make several comments on the lines of 'Ben is such a happy boy', 'Ben has a lovely smile' and 'Ben, you are so positive. You make me feel happy.' If, in spite of your prompts, a particular child fails to be put forward for consideration, you can always make use of your teacher nomination.

The name of the chosen child is written on the board and, at the end of the week, you check that the class agrees that the nominee has lived up to their nomination. If so, the nominee is presented with a sticker, or another reward of your choice. They could choose from whom they would like to receive the sticker. If the consensus is that the nominee has had difficulty living up to their nomination on this occasion, allow the child two further days to try to fulfil the criterion named.

Whole-class rewards

Whole-class reward schemes are a good way to promote pro-social behaviour. Within the Quality Circle Time model we use a whole-school reward system called Golden Time; the loss of Golden Time is an effective consequence for most children. Golden Time is a celebration for all the children who have kept the school's values – the Golden Rules – for a week. It is normally an hour each week when work stops and each child who has kept the rules can take part in exciting activities. Golden Time reinforces the expectation that children will keep to the rules for the week and arrive at Golden Time with their time intact. For those who break the rules there are systems whereby they can earn back some of their lost Golden Time, depending on their offence. For details see Mosley and Sonnet, *Better Behaviour through Golden Time* (2005), in the Resources section (page 32).

A wall display that is gradually filled in to show how quickly a class is progressing towards a goal provides both encouragement and finally a reward for the whole class. It also helps maintain a continued focus. The children love the anticipation of watching the display grow until they are eligible for their reward, which could be a disco, watching a DVD or some other event. You could incorporate a special occasion for the term into the scheme and use it as the reward. It is a good idea to change the incentive each term with the children's input. Two ideas for a cumulative incentive scheme follow:

☆ In a trees of kindness display, each tree needs eight leaves and three apples. These are gained for acts of kindness. You may decide that ten complete trees earn the children their reward. Children could decorate the leaves and apples to give a greater visual impact.

☆ In a garden of good sitting display, each sunflower needs a brown centre, eight petals, a stem and two leaves. These flower parts are gained for effective sitting and listening skills. You can decide how many flowers are needed to make the garden complete.

Keep the component parts for displays in a box, instructing the children to take the next as they earn it and add it to the display. Each tree or flower must be completed before a new one can be started. To use the scheme in subsequent years, laminate the parts.

There is a wealth of ideas for different scenes that you can build up in this way. The preparation may seem labour intensive, but once the components have been made, they can be used again.

Some whole-class schemes are rewards in themselves. The Helpful Tree is a sturdy twig secured in a pot with modelling clay. The twig can be painted gold to heighten its appeal. You need a collection of leaves made from card, each with a hole and a loop of string or wool through it. When a child has helped you or another child in the class, write their name and the deed on a leaf, and the child hangs it onto a branch. For example, 'Jay was helpful when he tidied the books' and 'Cara was helpful when she picked the pencils up from the floor.' You can show the children how the tree is flourishing because of their helpfulness.

Similar schemes use card bricks to build a wall of kindness, or hexagons to create a beehive of industry, through which the children are rewarded for trying hard.

Using rewards to help change behaviour

It takes a huge amount of effort to change behaviour. You are probably aware of this on account of the failed new year's resolutions that you've made in the past. If you consider the enormous task involved in asking children to change, perhaps without the help and support of their family, you will begin to understand what a massive undertaking this can be.

When you ask a child to change specific, often difficult, aspects of their behaviour, you need to show them that you appreciate how much effort they are making by giving them commensurate rewards.

The most effective way to proceed with such a child is to plan a programme with them that details the required changes needed to alter a particular aspect of behaviour. This should be as specific as possible – for example, to sit quietly on the carpet without interrupting when the teacher is speaking for five minutes, or to be gentle at playtime on Friday and not hurt other children physically.

It is best to work with the child to find out what might help them to achieve their target. This could be sitting next to a responsible child or keeping to a certain area at playtime. The days need to be broken up into manageable chunks of time, and your expectations must be realistic. We call them Tiny, Achievable, Tickable

Targets. To achieve a percentage of the target behaviour, the child has to be good enough to start with.

The reward has to be attractive enough to the child to make their effort worthwhile. It might be something like helping in the school library or a class of younger children. You will need to talk this through with the child to find something that appeals to them. You need to bear in mind that the reward may have to be changed regularly, because once it has been experienced it may lose its power of motivation.

You can encourage the rest of the children to help a child with their targeted behaviour by agreeing on a class reward that all will share in if a child fulfils their target. The other children then gain from helping the child, rather than being tempted to wind them up and see what trouble can be created.

It may take time and persistence for a child to respond to rewards and praise. Some children are so used to negative feedback that they feel uncomfortable with praise. When you tell them that they are doing well, they may immediately revert to the safety of their negative patterns of behaviour. In these instances, don't give up. If you observe this pattern of behaviour, try limiting the praise you offer, just reporting back to the child the specific behaviour you are pleased with until they are comfortable with their new, more positive self.

Occasionally, we encounter a child who is beyond the normal motivational reward systems in school. This is a child who has been given many opportunities to attain acceptable levels of behaviour, without success. Such 'children beyond' deserve and require specialist input. For details see Mosley, *Quality Circle Time* (1996) and *More Quality Circle Time* (1998) (page 32).

Including parents or carers in your reward schemes

Utilising parent or carer power, especially with reference to a behaviour-modification programme, can be a great asset and an important source of support. Parents or carers can be involved by giving their child an agreed reward at home if they reach the required target at school. If you can persuade them to offer a reward such as playing a game with their child, reading a book to them or going on a small outing together, the home reward will be more helpful than a new toy or some

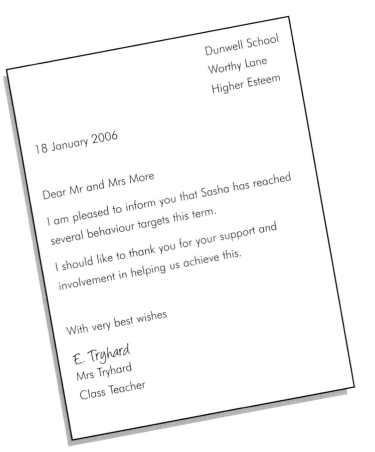

Dunwell School
Worthy Lane
Higher Esteem

18 January 2006

Dear Mr and Mrs More

I am pleased to inform you that Sasha has reached several behaviour targets this term.

I should like to thank you for your support and involvement in helping us achieve this.

With very best wishes

E. Tryhard
Mrs Tryhard
Class Teacher

sweets – it has the added bonus of quality time spent together. This is often viewed as a very special reward and may be highly motivational. It also actively involves the parents or carers in the programme you have set up for the child, so they are more likely to be focused in their encouragement.

It is beneficial to show your appreciation of the parents' or carers' efforts by sending them a special thank-you letter for their support. Where the lifestyle and behaviour of the parents or carers are contributory factors to the child's inappropriate behaviour in school, you are, in effect, asking them to try to change as well. Acknowledging that you are aware of their positive intentions and efforts can be a great encouragement to keep up the good work at home as it is really helping the child reach their targets in school. See page 26 for an example.

Involving parents may seem daunting, but if you approach them with consideration, give value to their opinions, gain their trust and demonstrate that you have their child's best interests at heart, you will find them a major source of support and information.

Rewards at playtime and lunchtime

Playtimes and lunchtimes are potential opportunities for problems to arise as the children have more freedom and are less supervised then. Rewards are therefore especially important during these times to keep the children on track and behaving well.

Lunchtime supervisors need to be given access to customised stickers celebrating good behaviour. They could also award mini-certificates on which they tick the behaviour for which they are commending the child. Some schools link these with their classroom incentives, so a mini-certificate at lunchtime might be worth a merit or class-team point. Some teachers display the certificates on their class boards before the children take them home.

I am pleased with you, because you chose to:
1. show good manners
2. be helpful
3. refuse to be drawn into a fight
4. play well with other children
5. queue patiently
6. ask someone to join in a game.

Date

Special lunchtime certificates can be awarded during a whole-school assembly to children who have behaved well all term, celebrating their ability to keep the rules (see page 32 for a reference to LDA's version).

In some schools, raffle tickets are handed out by the lunchtime supervisors to children who are behaving well. The children take their tickets to the end-of-week assembly. The other half is placed in a container, and during the assembly the head teacher picks one or two tickets. The children with the matching halves receive a clap from the whole school (or a suitable prize).

The Special Dining Table is a great way to encourage good manners in the dining hall. A table is decked out with a tablecloth, place mats and a small vase of flowers.

Children who display good manners in the dining hall are selected to eat at this table for one day or a week. Those selected can choose a friend to join them on the table. Supervisors remind the children while they are eating that they will be looking out for suitable candidates to sit at this table on the next occasion. During a Circle Time you can talk about what constitutes good manners while eating, and even let the children role play going to a restaurant so that they can practise their manners and polite conversation.

Lunchtime Certificate

Congratulations

Sharmina

you have kept the Lunchtime Rules

★ We play well with others
★ We care for the playground
★ We remember to use good table manners
★ We put our rubbish in the bin
★ We line up calmly
    ll adults

Looking online

There is a wealth of information about rewards online. For example, if you go into www.google.co.uk and type in 'rewards for children in school', you will find pages of websites to browse. Many are from schools detailing their successful reward systems. Spend a little time typing in different subjects to see what comes up.

You will find plenty of good-practice advice at www.circle-time.co.uk, along with details of Jenny Mosley's work in schools.

Visit www.superstickers.com to look at their products and benefit from online savings.

Conclusion

When we are young, we build our self-concept from the feedback we receive from the people around us. If we believe that we are clever, sociable or fun to be with, we do so because someone smiled, enjoyed our company and told us so. Similarly, children who think themselves stupid, useless or ugly hold that belief because other people cause them to feel that way.

Once we have acquired a concept of ourselves, we allow it to affect our attitude to everything we think, feel and do. A child who believes they are clever is motivated and confident and very likely to prove themselves right, whereas another child who believes they are stupid will have a negative attitude before your lesson has even begun.

For this reason, it is vital that the adults who surround each child make a sustained and consistent effort: to make absolutely sure that every child in their care receives enough strengthening feedback to develop the self-concept of a person who believes that they are capable and worthy of success, and of all the good things that life has to offer. In all of this, don't forget to reward yourself too.

As teachers, you have many strategies at your disposal. You build supportive relationships with your class; you give clear guidelines so that everyone knows what is expected of them; you show respect for your children's feelings and opinions; you use teaching methods that involve and interest your class and teach them according to their preferred learning styles; and, importantly, you reward the behaviours that you wish to reinforce.

The danger with rewards is that they can be seen by children as a method of controlling their behaviour rather than a means of enhancing their personal engagement in a given task. Remember that rewards are not bribes that buy a child's good behaviour but instead reinforce their desire to maintain that behaviour in the future.

This book shows you how to use rewards as a form of tangible praise. When used in this wise way, rewards enable a child to touch, keep, show and tell your praise beyond the confines of your classroom. When you approach reward-giving in the ways explained, you are making sure that your children feel that their success is valuable enough to merit the recognition it has received and to 'show the world' joyfully, not just today but for many days to come. This strengthens their self-concept and gives them the motivation to strive for more success. And what could feel better than that?

Resources

Mosley, J. (1993) *Turn your School Round*

Mosley, J. (1996) *Quality Circle Time*

Mosley, J. (1998) *More Quality Circle Time*

Mosley, J. (2005) *Successful Lunchtimes for Supervisors*

Mosley, J. and Sonnet, H. (2005) *Better Behaviour through Golden Time*

Mosley, J. and Thorp, G. (2005) *Positive Playtimes*

Mosley, J. (1996) *Responsibility Badges*

Mosley, J. (2000) *Quality Circle Time in Action*

Mosley, J. (2000) *Quality Circle Time Kit*

Mosley, J. (2004) *Circle Time Stickers*

Mosley, J. (2004) *Golden Rules Stickers*

Mosley, J. (2004) *Lunchtimes Stickers*

Mosley, J. (2004) *Circle Time Certificates*

Mosley, J. (2004) *Golden Rules Certificates*

Mosley, J. (2004) *Lunchtime Certificates*

Mosley, J. (2005) *Classroom Poster Set*

Mosley, J. (2005) *Golden Rules Poster Set*

Mosley, J. (2005) *Lunchtime Poster Set*

Mosley, J. (2005) *Playground Stars*

Mosley, J. and Thorp, G. (2002) *Playground Notelets*

All these resources are published in Cambridge by LDA. For information about the full range of Jenny Mosley's books and resources, please contact LDA Customer Services on 0845 120 4776 or visit our website at www.LDAlearning.com

For information about SuperStickers, contact:

Telephone: 0800 318192

Fax: 0800 027 2833

Website: www.superstickers.com

Training in the Quality Circle Time model

For information about training, contact Jenny Mosley Consultancies:

Telephone: 01225 767157

E-mail: circletime@jennymosley.co.uk

Website: www.circle-time.co.uk

Write to: 28a Gloucester Road, Trowbridge, Wiltshire, BA14 0AA

Reference

Harrop, A. and Swinson, J. (2005) 'An examination of the effects of a short course aimed at enabling teachers in infant, junior and secondary schools to alter the verbal feedback given to their pupils' *Educational Studies*, 4, 2, pp108–111